THE SUMERIANS' WRITING SYSTEM AND LITERATURE

Ancient History Books 5th Grade

Children's Ancient History

Speedy Publishing LLC

40 E. Main St. #1156

Newark, DE 19711

www.speedypublishing.com

Copyright 2017

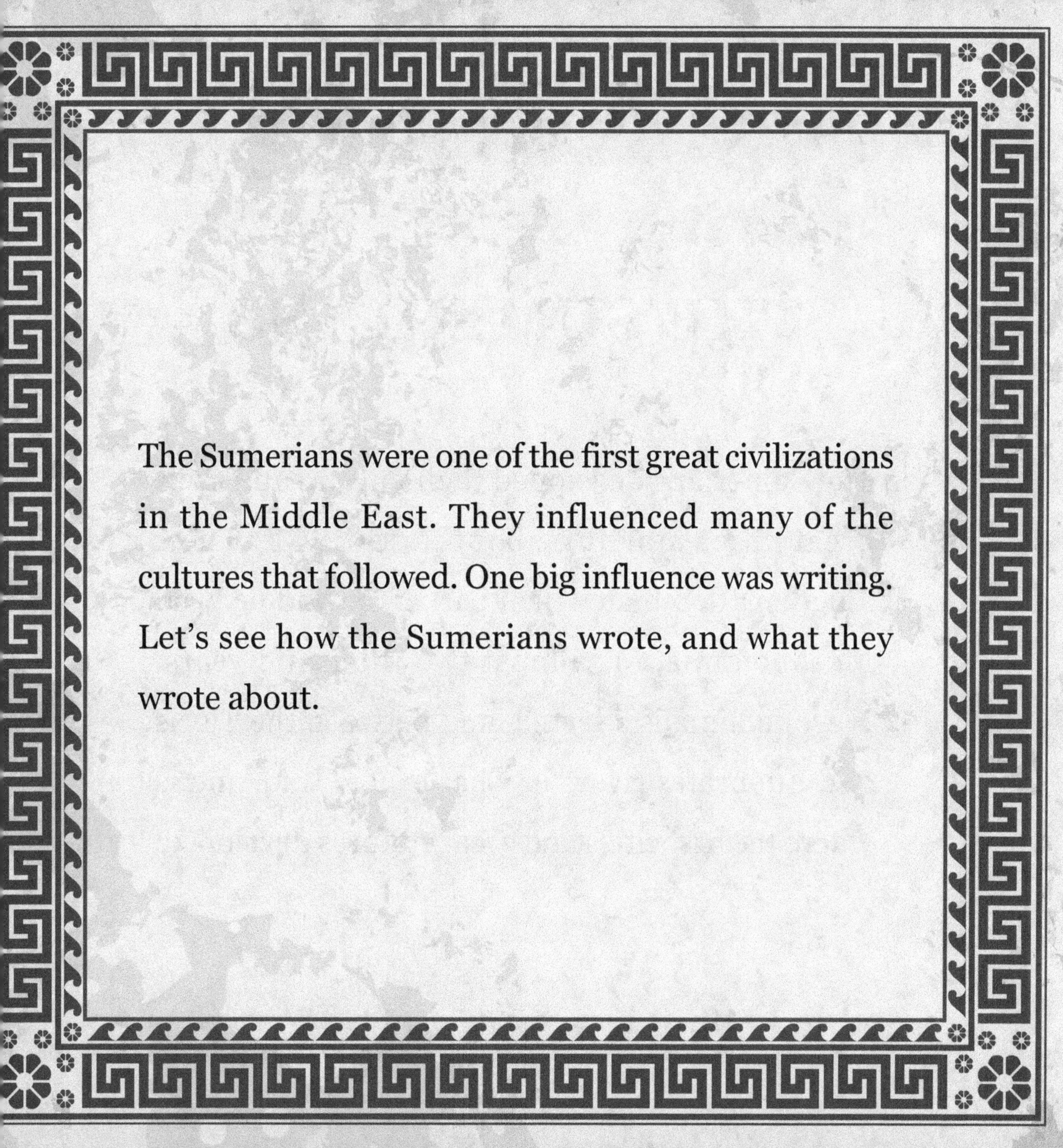

The Sumerians were one of the first great civilizations in the Middle East. They influenced many of the cultures that followed. One big influence was writing. Let's see how the Sumerians wrote, and what they wrote about.

THE SUMERIANS

The Sumerians developed their culture and their great cities starting about 4,500 BCE. Their kingdoms dominated their part of the Middle East, Mesopotamia, for almost two thousand years.

Mesopotamia is a fertile land between the Tigris and Euphrates rivers in what is now Iraq, and is where the first cities and great cultures developed.

Tigris River

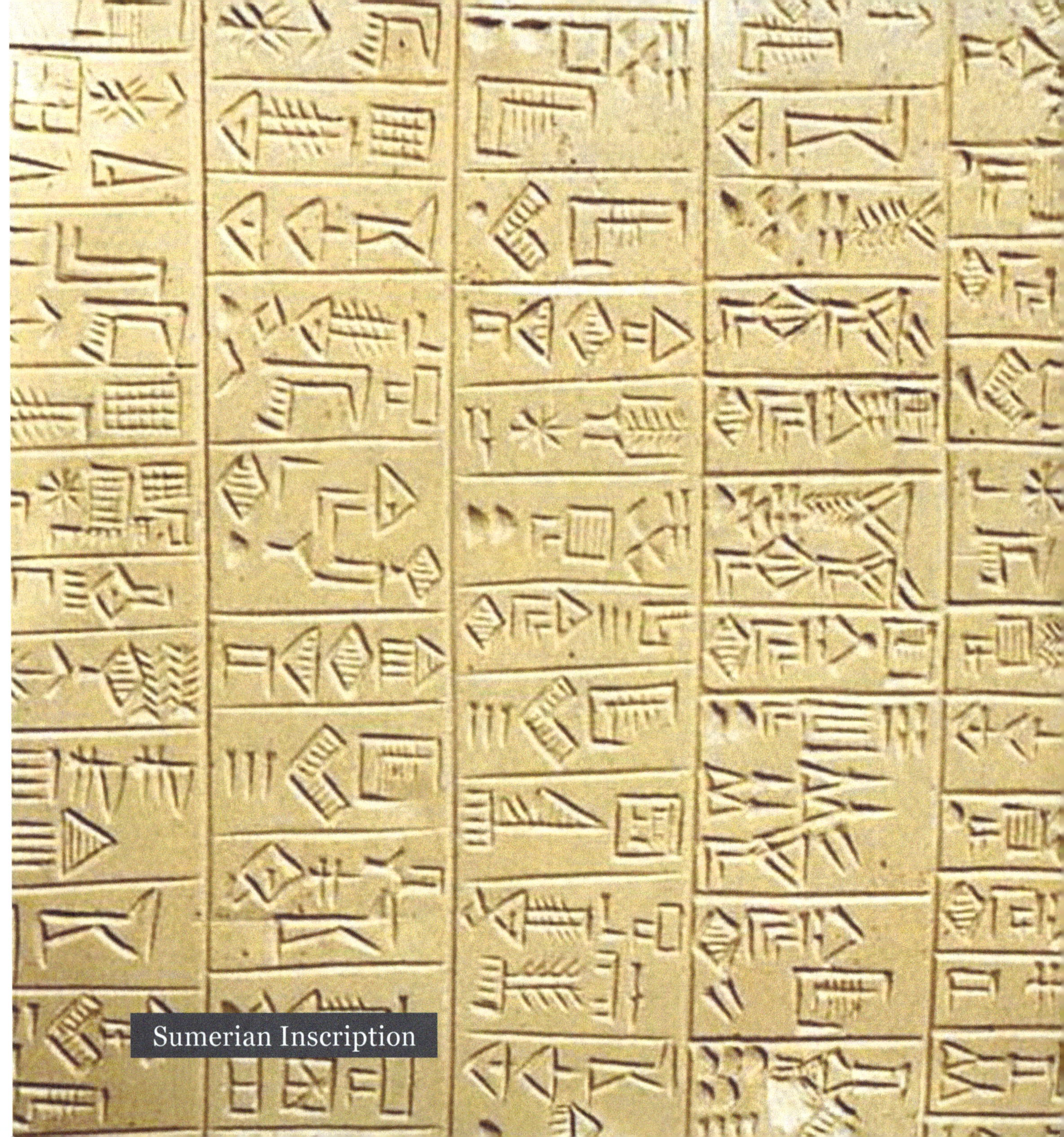
Sumerian Inscription

DEVELOPING WRITING

People in the ancient Middle East, as they developed cities and commerce and the idea of wealth, had to develop a way to keep track of things. How many cattle did I give you last month, and how much wheat did you say you were going to give me next month? It's easy to lose track of things if you have not figured out how to write stuff down.

At one point the Sumerians used clay objects, like pieces for a board game. Different shaped objects meant different types of things. To keep the objects from getting mixed up or stolen, they would put the objects related to a single transaction in a clay tube, and seal that up.

Sumerian Tablet

But, oops, what if we forget how many objects are in the tube? To avoid having to break the tubes open, they started pressing images of the clay objects on the outside of the tube. Three little triangle shapes on this tube means there are three little triangles inside. Each triangle could represent a cow, or a wagon-load of grain, or a pair of sandals.

A while after that, the Sumerians realized they didn't need the tubes and the objects at all! All they needed were the marks! So they started pressing marks into wet clay tablets, and very soon instead of making seven triangle marks they figured out that they could make a single triangle mark plus a mark meaning "seven of these things". Writing in Mesopotamia had developed this far by about 3000 BCE.

Clay Tablet

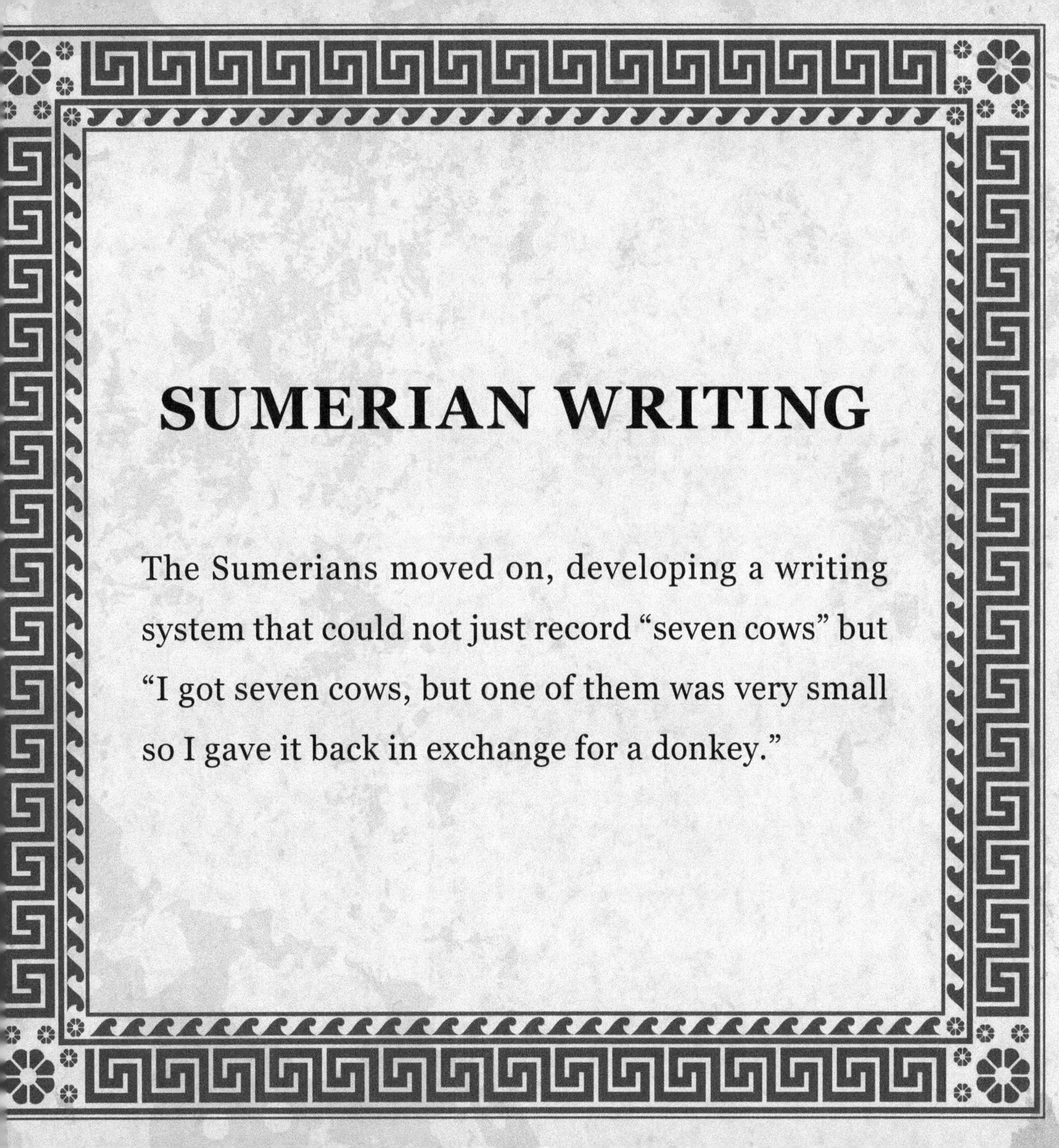

SUMERIAN WRITING

The Sumerians moved on, developing a writing system that could not just record "seven cows" but "I got seven cows, but one of them was very small so I gave it back in exchange for a donkey."

Originally, Sumerian writing was written to be read from top to bottom. Then, around 3000 BCE, it started being written left to right across the the tablet. Around the same time the system settled on its distinctive mark, a wedge shape, instead of the older form that involved straight and curved lines. Multiple wedge shapes would form a single character. We don't know why the system changed like that.

Tablet with Cylinder Seal

Sumerian Clay Tablet

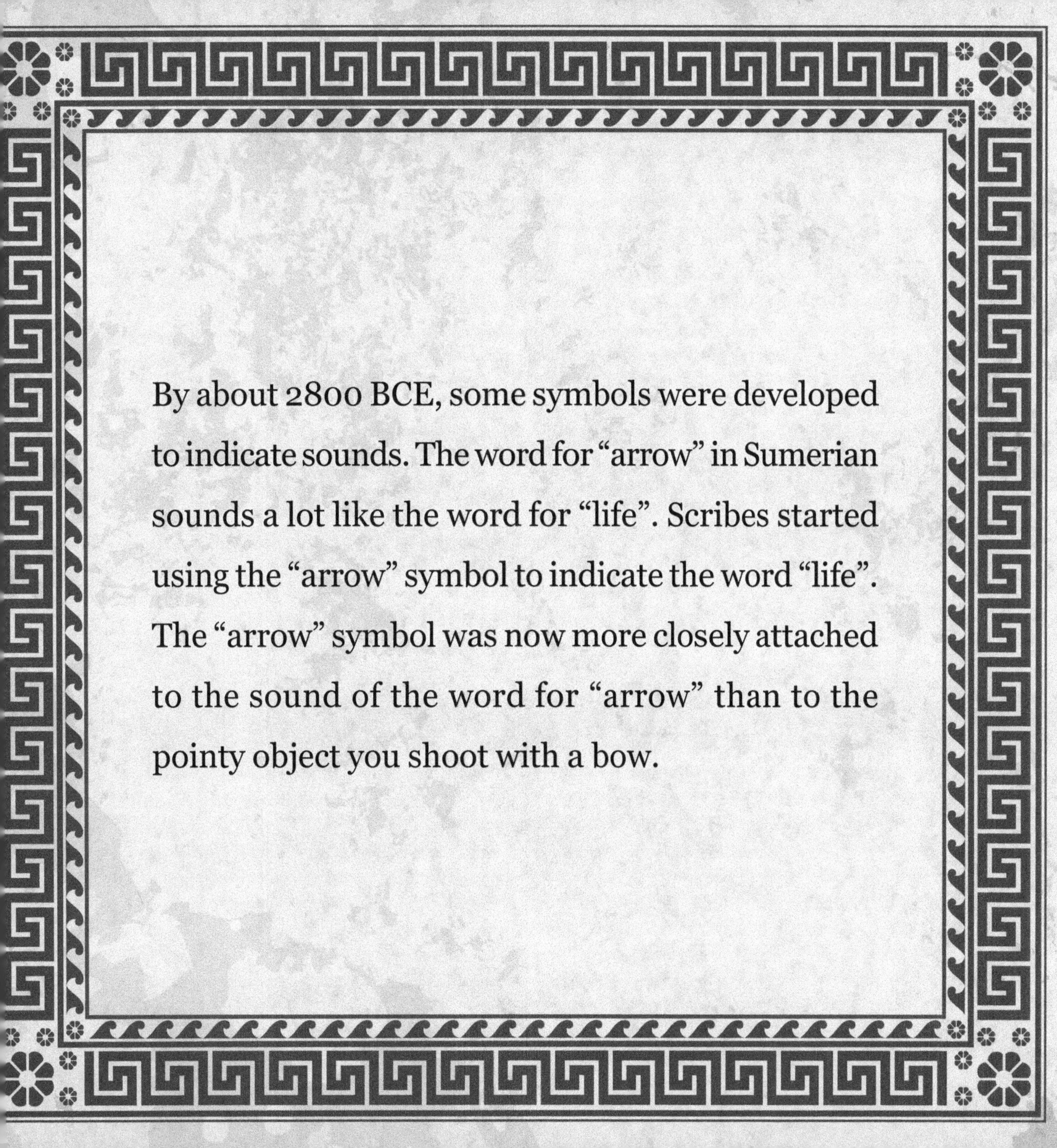

By about 2800 BCE, some symbols were developed to indicate sounds. The word for "arrow" in Sumerian sounds a lot like the word for "life". Scribes started using the "arrow" symbol to indicate the word "life". The "arrow" symbol was now more closely attached to the sound of the word for "arrow" than to the pointy object you shoot with a bow.

There was no general agreement, as the language developed, about which word's symbol should be the one to represent a common sound, and different scribes made different choices when they were writing words that had many syllables, and that needed symbols for many sounds.

Sumerian Clay Tablet

Sumerians

Take the sound "guh": Sumerian writers used more than ten different symbols for words (as varied as "voice", "neck", and "flax") that sounded sort of like "guh" to represent the sound "guh" when they were writing more complex words that had "guh" in them! As you can imagine, it took a lot of study to be able to read what some other scribe had written!

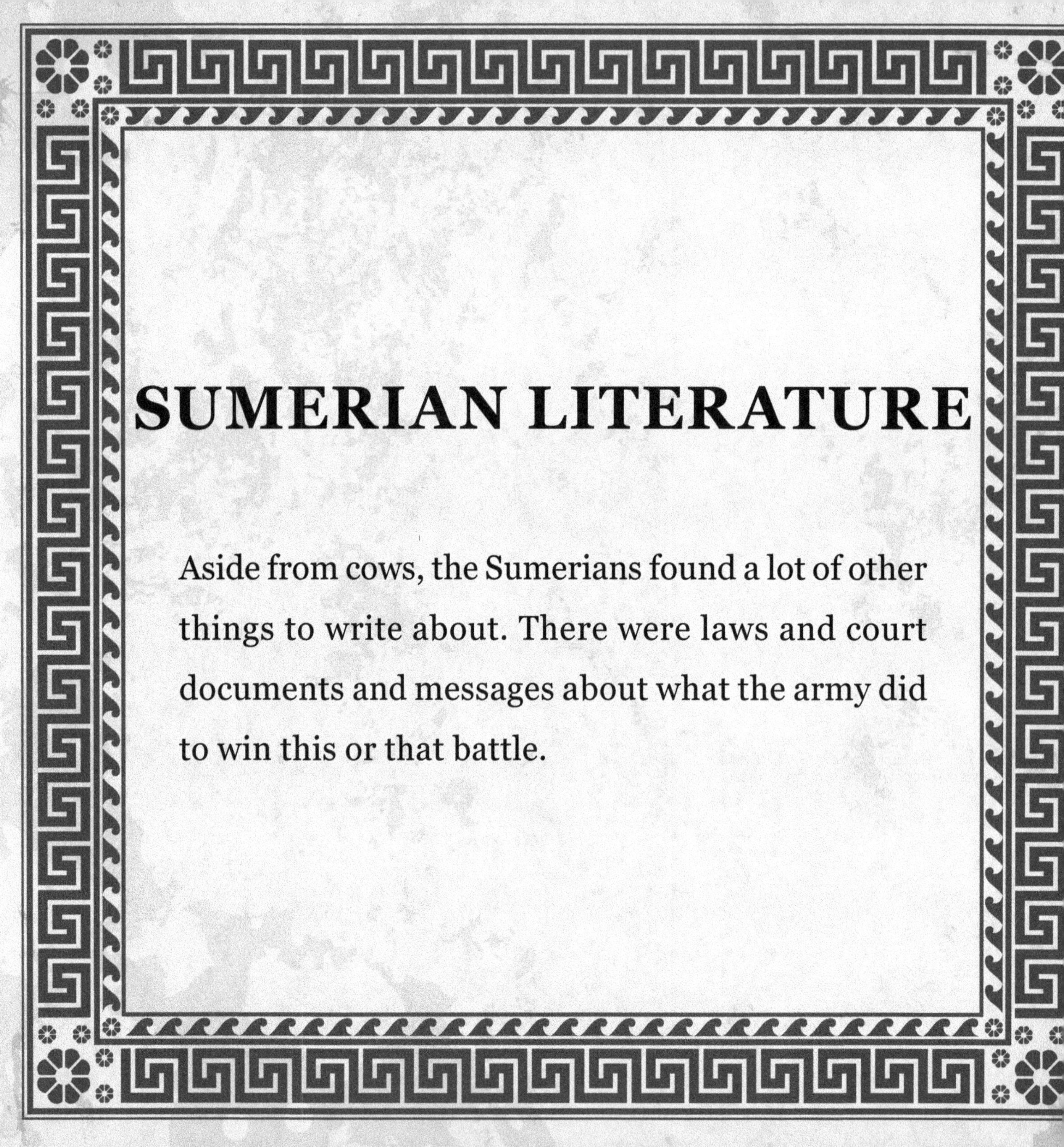

SUMERIAN LITERATURE

Aside from cows, the Sumerians found a lot of other things to write about. There were laws and court documents and messages about what the army did to win this or that battle.

Sumerian Writing

But some of the most interesting Sumerian writing is their stories and poems. These items are written with the first character of each line lined up at the left side of the tablet, and they seem to follow certain writing rules the way rhyming poetry in English follows rules about lines, rhymes, and verses. But beyond that we don't know the rules of Sumerian poetry.

After the Akkadians became dominant in the region, Akkadian was the language of most business and day-to-day communication. Sumerian became the language of scholars and literary writers. Sumerian was to the ancient Middle East what Latin was to Europe from about 500 to 1700 CE: a common language learned by thinkers and scholars in many nations for sharing important ideas.

Akkadians

Tablet of the Epic of Gilgamesh

Sumerian literature had a great influence on the writing of many civilizations in Mesopotamia, including Babylon and the Persian Empire. Of the Sumerian literature that remains, there some famous examples:

- A story of the creation of the world and a Great Flood, like the stories at the beginning of the Bible.
- Stories about the adventures of the goddess Inanna.
- Stories of the battles and adventures of King Enmerkar of Uruk. This collection includes the story of the building of a great tower, and the failure of the project, like the story of the Tower of Babel in the Bible.
- The Epic of Gilgamesh, on twelve clay tablets.

GILGAMESH

The most famous Sumerian document is "The Epic of Gilgamesh". It is one of the earliest examples of literary writing (about a story or a feeling or an idea, instead of about how many cows got sold).

Gilgamesh Statue

GILGAMESH, ASSYRIAN KING OF URUK DURING THE THIRD MILLENIUM BC, IS PART GOD AND PART MAN. HE SETS OUT ON A QUEST TO SEEK IMMORTALITY. IN THE COURSE OF HIS QUEST, HE FINDS COMPASSION, FRIENDSHIP, COURAGE, LOVE AND PEACE.

IN THE 19TH CENTURY, SIR AUSTEN HENRY LAYARD FOUND CLAY TABLETS RECOUNTING THE EPIC OF GILGAMESH IN ASHOURBANIPAL'S 8TH CENTURY BC LIBRARY AT NINEVAH. THIS EPIC, ONE OF THE OLDEST WRITTEN STORIES, IS THE BASIS OF MANY MYTHS, LEGENDS AND TALES, INCLUDING MODERN ONES.

The Epic of Gilgamesh

The story is a series of adventures of Gilgamesh, the king of Uruk. Gilgamesh may have been an actual king in Sumerian history, but in the epic he is a being two-thirds a mortal and one-third a god. He is powerful, but he is limited in understanding some things humans understand, like kindness, because of being part-god.

The other main character is Enkidu, a man who is from a wild culture and is just learning to be civilized. Gilgamesh and Enkidu start as rivals and fight each other, but then become friends. In many ways, it is Gilgamesh who learns virtues like honesty and humility from Enkidu.

Enkidu

Gilgamesh and Enkidu

Once Gilgamesh and Enkidu are friends, they have a series of adventures. These include:

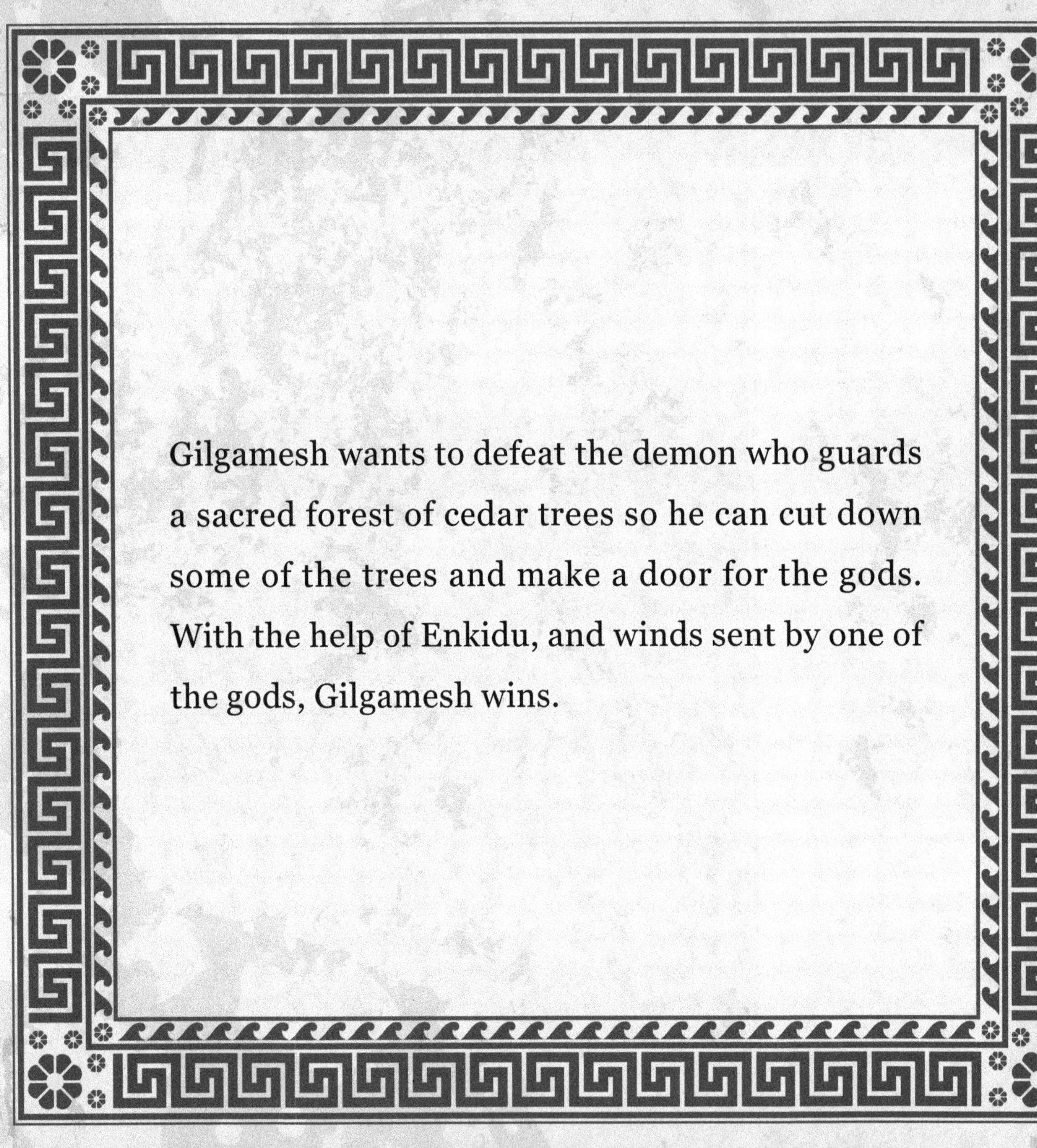

Gilgamesh wants to defeat the demon who guards a sacred forest of cedar trees so he can cut down some of the trees and make a door for the gods. With the help of Enkidu, and winds sent by one of the gods, Gilgamesh wins.

Gilgamesh

Fragments of Ishtar

Later, Ishtar, the goddess of love and war, is interested in Gilgamesh. He does not want anything to do with her, and this upsets her. Her father, the sky god, sends a monster to plague the land until Gilgamesh changes his mind. Gilgamesh and Enkidu manage to kill the monster.

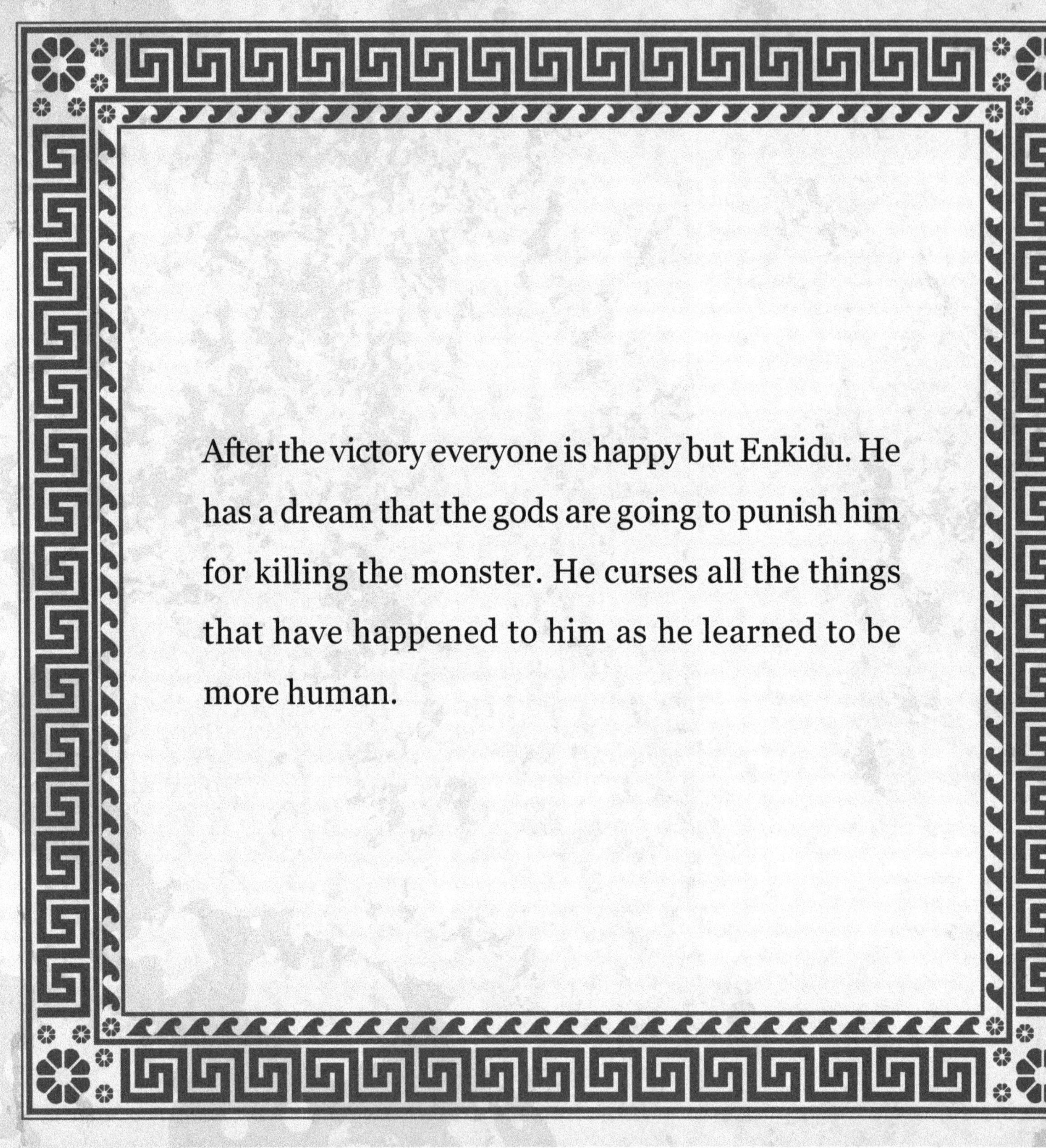

After the victory everyone is happy but Enkidu. He has a dream that the gods are going to punish him for killing the monster. He curses all the things that have happened to him as he learned to be more human.

Enkidu

Tablet V of the Epic of Gligamesh

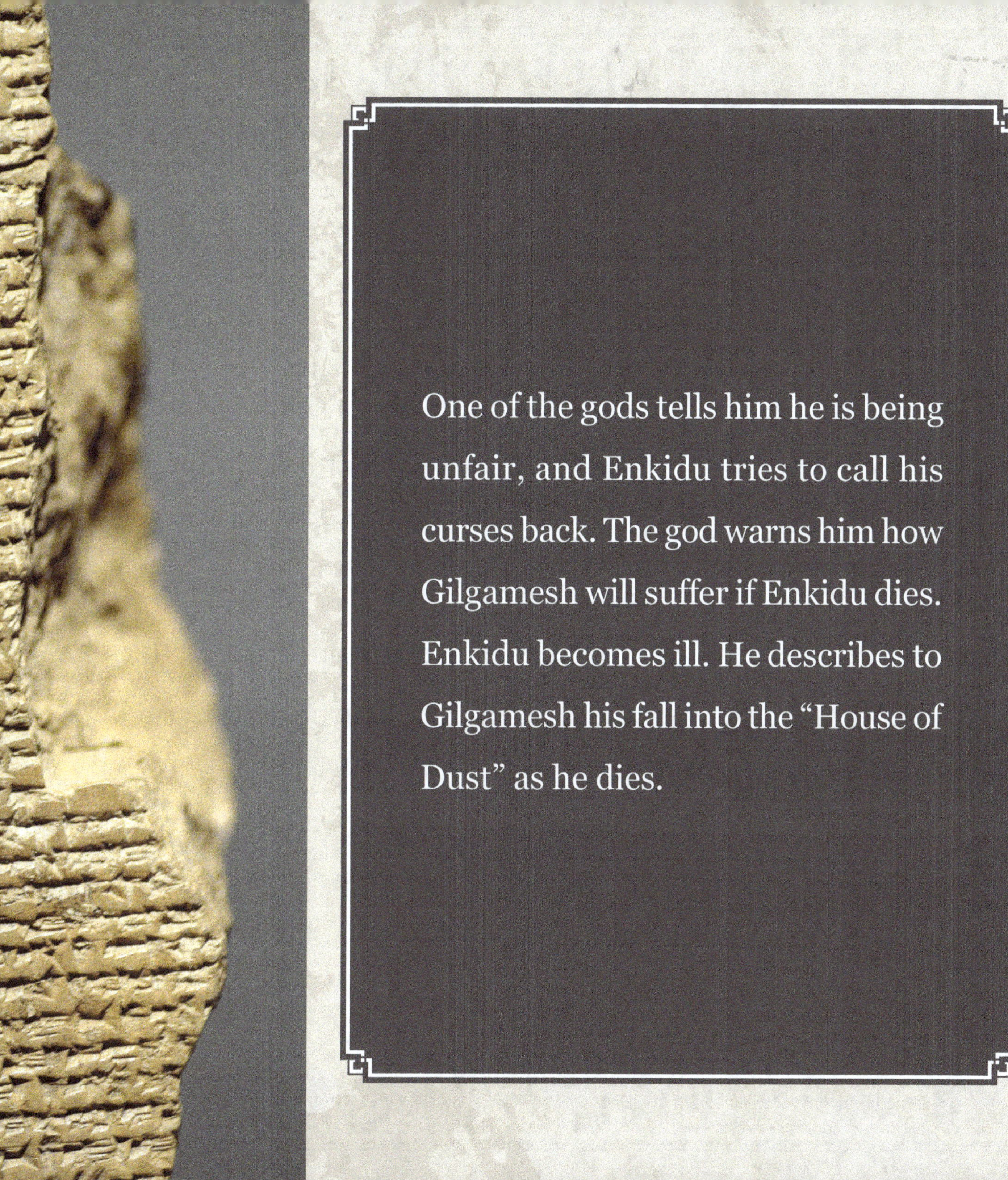

One of the gods tells him he is being unfair, and Enkidu tries to call his curses back. The god warns him how Gilgamesh will suffer if Enkidu dies. Enkidu becomes ill. He describes to Gilgamesh his fall into the "House of Dust" as he dies.

Gilgamesh is crushed by Enkidu's death. He tries to bribe the gods to let the two of them be back together. When this does not work, he decides to make a dangerous journey to visit the two humans who survived the Great Flood and who were made immortal by the gods. He wants to learn their secret of everlasting life.

Epic of Gilgamesh

Gilgamesh

Gilgamesh has to cross oceans and mountains, and fight monsters, to get to the people he needs to talk to. He meets people who either try to prevent him from going forward, or help him in his journey. On his way he gets help crossing the Sea of Death, that will kill anyone who touches it.

Gilgamesh finally meets Utnapishtim and his wife, the two humans who survived the Great Flood. He has further adventures while convincing them to help him in his quest. Utnapishtim offers to tell Gilgamesh the secret of eternal life, but the telling takes six days and seven nights and Gilgamesh falls asleep before Utnapishtim gets to the key bit!

The Flood Tablet

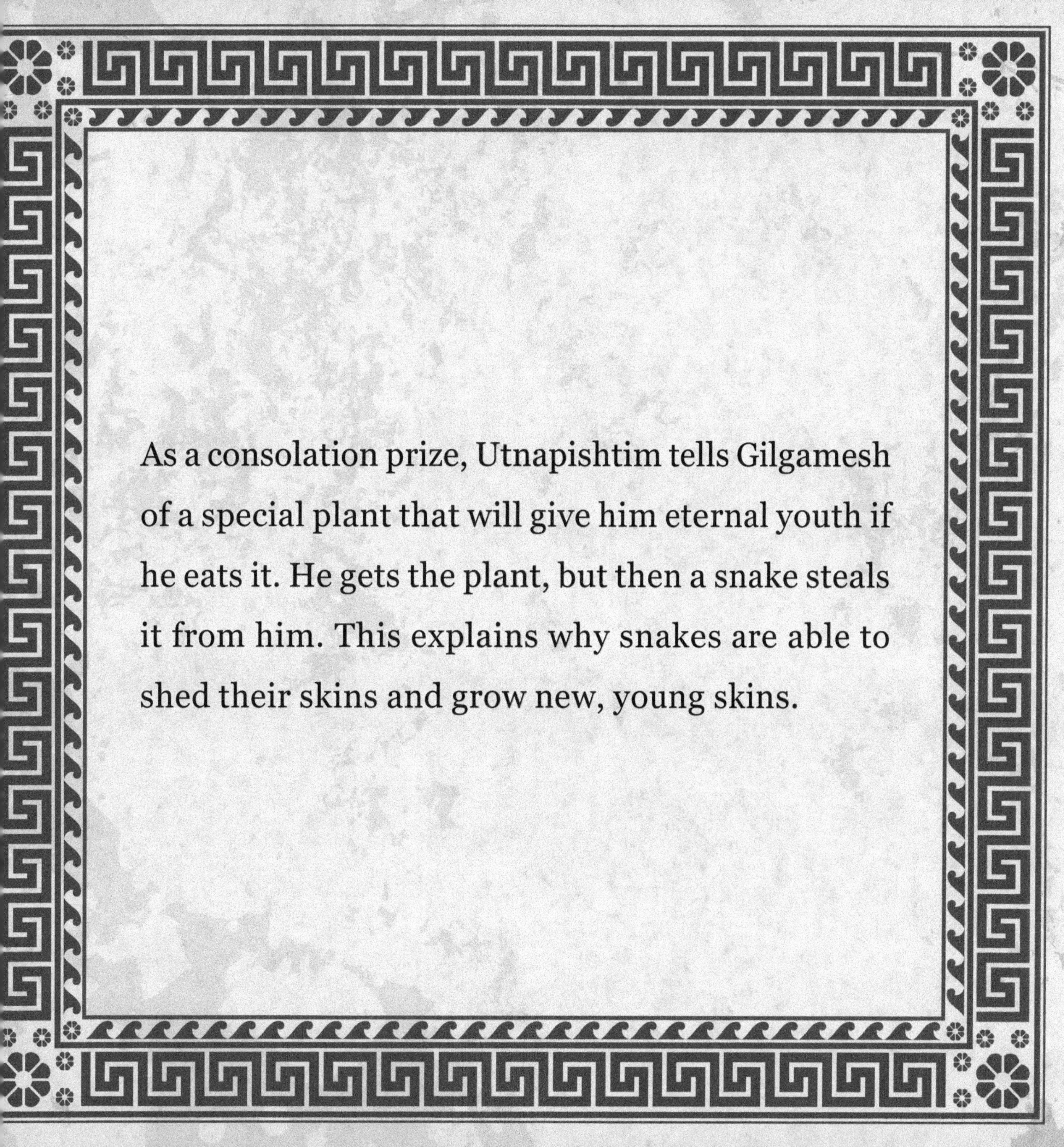

As a consolation prize, Utnapishtim tells Gilgamesh of a special plant that will give him eternal youth if he eats it. He gets the plant, but then a snake steals it from him. This explains why snakes are able to shed their skins and grow new, young skins.

"The Epic of Gilgamesh" is an ancient series of stories. Yet it tries to deal with questions of love, loyalty, what it means to be a person, and the search for eternal life.

Cuneiform Tablets Display

Mesopotamia
Samosata
Masius M.
Marde
Sapphe
Rezabde
Tela
(Antoninopolis)
Zabdicene
Dara
Azochis
Edessa
s. Orrhoë
Amudis
Sisaurana
Apamea
Nisibis
Osroëne
Doliche
Mygdonia
Zeugma
Anthemusias
Bithiga
(Sarug)
Bathnae
Carrhae
Ggdonia
Mygdonius F.
Europus
(Charan)
Resaina
Saocoras F.
(Carchemish)
Libana
barazа
Dabana
Thalaba
MESOPOTAMIA
Hierapolis
Thergubis
Thilsaphata
(Bambyce)
Chaboras F.
L. Beberaci
NI
Bethammaris
Thubida
Singara
(NI
Bathnae
Ichnae
Zama
Ur
Eublechas F.
Erazіga
Apammaris
Gauzanitis
Ur.
Barbalissus
Nicephorium
(Callinicum)
Arabes
Abhorrhas
Araxes
Thapsacus
Sura
Arabana
Hatra
Resapha
Zenobia
Appadang
Birtha
Phaliga
Oriza
Circesium
Catanii
Zaïtha
Cholle
Dura (Europus)
Araca
Belesibiblada
Anatho
Palmyra
Corsote
Rescipha
(Tadmor)
Giddan
Thilabus I.
DESERTA
Auranitis
Diacira
Is
(Charmar
B.
s.

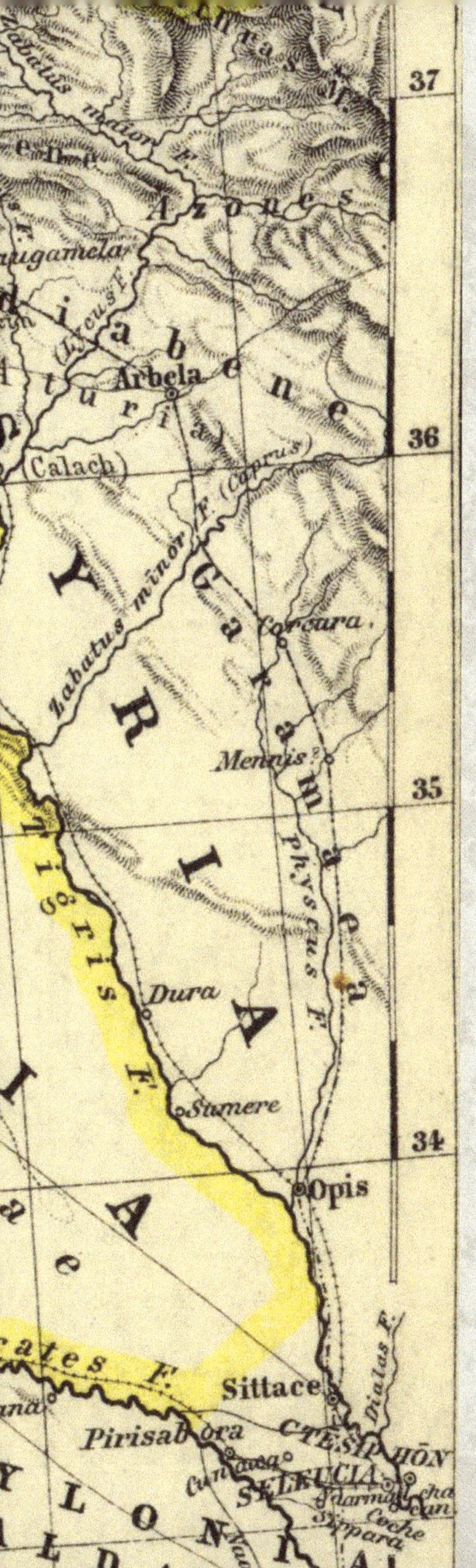

EXPLORE MESOPOTAMIA

Many civilizations and cultures developed, rose to power, and then fell in Mesopotamia.

THE SUMERIANS' WRITING SYSTEM AND LITERATURE CONTRIBUTION TO THE WORLD

Writing and reading thousands of years ago was only for the privileged members of the elite class and scribes. That is why not everyone knows how to read the ancient writings.

The Sumerians have greatly influenced today's writing system, them being one of the earliest urban societies that existed. The Cuneiform script was one of the most historical contribution that they imparted to civilization.

There's more to learn about The Sumerians like their Art, Religion and way of life. Read thru from other Baby Professor books to find out!

Mesopotamia

Visit

BABY PROFESSOR
EDUCATION KIDS

www.BabyProfessorBooks.com

to download Free Baby Professor eBooks and view
our catalog of new and exciting Children's Books